Y...

AUTHORS
OF
AMERICA

☆

VOLUME TWO

1988

YOUNG AUTHORS OF AMERICA

☆

VOLUME TWO

1988

Edited and With an Introduction by
Ellen Rudin

Published by
The Trumpet Club
666 Fifth Avenue
New York, New York 10103

ISBN: 0-440-84206-9

Printed in the United States of America
January 1989

10 9 8 7 6 5 4 3 2 1
OPM

CONTENTS

INTRODUCTION

In its second year, the Trumpet Club's Young Authors of America Contest drew an astonishing response—more than 7000 manuscripts, well over twice the number received in 1987, enough to keep us busy reading all summer long.

Every entry gave insight into a young mind, and very many of them were outstanding. It was not an easy job to judge "the best," but in the end first, second, and third place winners were chosen, along with ten runners-up. All thirteen manuscripts are published in this volume. As well, the work of one hundred and fifteen other young writers, whose names are listed at the back of this book, received honorable mention in the contest.

Except when creating fantasy, and there was plenty of that, this year's participants overwhelmingly favored themes close to them. No fewer than five of the winning stories, for example, take place in school or on the way to it, and all but two involve either family relationships or friendships.

Among all the manuscripts, pets and other animals appeared frequently, as did grandparents. Having to move to a new place was a big concern.

Fantasy took the form often of encounters with alien life and trips in time machines, as well as experiences with such fabulous creatures as elves, trolls, wizards, and unicorns. Another kind of fantasy, dreams, was expressed in the frequent wish for achievement and wealth. There were a lot of lottery winners in these stories! Themes of mystery and detection, terror and horror, and spirits, appeared and reappeared like ghosts themselves.

The winning manuscripts, together, are all entertaining to read, and they offer perceptive child's-eye views of many of life's larger issues. In "Angel" by Ian B. DeMeritt a boy obsessed by his horse seeks for reasons why the horse had to die. Chris Joplin's hilarious "The Weirdest Dream of My Life . . . Part III" convinces us that its hero, reduced permanently to the size of a grasshopper, will be able to carry on. "Kate Did It" by Eileen Markey passionately describes the positive influence of one girl on a whole class. "Brotherly Love" by J. S. Eldridge tells of his family's joy in adopting a baby. Two internal monologues—"Awful Day" by Michiko Hanao and "Days on the Bus" by Ron Riske, Jr.—capture the misery and pain of personal situations so feelingly that readers will easily identify with them. In a very funny story, "The Talking Iguana" by Andrew Eric Harrison, a boy wishes for an extraordinary pet and later wishes the same pet, now unwanted, on someone else. A show-off fish befriends a boy in J. J. Donohue's "My Fishy Friends," and a farmer outsmarts three clever barnyard birds in "The Farmer's Choice" by Johnny Quiñones. With straightfaced humor, Mario Demasi describes an unexpectedly endless walk in "My Trip to School." The book's only poem, "A Wintery Day" by Luci Crawford, lyrically catches the special mood of that season. In "Growing Up" Naomi Anne Schaefer passes along to readers some of the insights she has learned the hard way on her own. "They Called It Dare Mountain" by Amanda J. Sullivan follows four friends on a mountain climbing adventure that, despite tragedy, ends in triumph.

"Ronda is a tall girl, 4 feet, 7 inches," one young contestant wrote in her story. Perspective—it's all in how one looks at things. Out of 7,343 entries, 13—or one in 565—made it to this book. Looked at from another perspective, more than 7000 boys and girls wrote manuscripts and sent them to the contest. That is a tremendous achievement.

ELLEN RUDIN
October 1988

ANGEL

by

Ian B. DeMeritt

Chapter 1
A Visitor

"Dad, someone's here!" yelled Tom as he ran through the door.

"OK, Son, I'll be down in a minute," said Dad from the second story of the Johnsons' farmhouse. Tom and his dad had lived on the farm ever since Tom's mother had died seven years before in a tragic automobile accident. They lived with Shep, their collie; three goats; two cows; and a number of chickens.

"Dad, someone's here!" repeated Tom. By this time, the stranger was at the door.

Tom had first seen the man drive up the road in his black, shiny Rolls Royce when he had just come out of the barn after milking and feeding the cows, goats, and chickens. Tom had never seen such a fancy car in his life. He and his dad had to walk everywhere because they did not have enough money to afford a car. But the weird thing about it, Tom had thought, is that a fancy car is pulling a horse trailer. He had set down the pail of milk he was carrying and run to the house to tell his dad. It was not very often that they received visitors.

Chapter 2
The Stranger

When Dad came down, the stranger was sitting on the couch in the living room with Tom. The stranger looked rich. He had on a suit and wore a neatly trimmed moustache. When Dad walked into the room, the stranger stood and shook hands with him.

"Howdy, name's Gary Smith," said the man. "Call me Gary."

"Hello, Gary. My name is Tim Johnson and this is my son, Tom. What brings you to these parts?"

"Well," said Gary, "it's sort of a long story."

Chapter 3
The Story

"Start from the beginning," said Dad. So Gary began.

"I come from an estate in Virginia. My father owned it, but he passed away a few months ago. He had written in his will that I could have half of his money if I sold a certain horse that he had on his estate."

"Is that wh—"? started Tom.

"Ah, don't butt into a conversation like that, Tom. You'll find out," said Gary. "Where was I? Oh, yes. As I was saying, he wanted me to sell a colt he had, so I came down to this part of the country and put ads in all the newspapers. One day I got a response. The lady that answered my ad didn't want to buy the colt, but she told me about you, knowing that you have a farm and no horses. To make a long story short, here I am."

Chapter 4
The Colt

"Can we take a look at him?" asked Dad.

"It's a her, and she's in the trailer hitched to the car," said Gary. "Come on." As the three guys walked through the door, Tom wondered what the horse would look like, how much it would cost, and whether his dad would buy it.

"Well, here we are," said Gary, opening the trailer door. There, standing quietly inside the trailer, was the ugliest horse Tom had ever seen. It had dirty, white, uncombed hair that looked like it hadn't been groomed for months, and it was so skinny you could see its ribs.

"How much are you asking for her?" asked Dad.

"One hundred dollars."

Dad laughed. "One hundred dollars for that bag of bones?"

"Wait," said Tom. "Mr. Smith said all he had to do was sell the horse to get half of his father's money. So if he would be kind enough to drop the price to fifteen dollars, I'll buy her."

"Now, Son," said Dad. "Are you sure you're doing the right thing?"

"I'm positive!" said Tom.

Chapter 5
A Horse for a Kid

After Dad had given his approval to buy the horse, Tom ran up to his room to empty his piggy bank. As the coins were falling out, Tom almost put them back, remembering all the hard work and time he had spent earning and saving the money. Now it would all go into something that might not even be worth five cents. But Tom figured that to him it would be more than fifteen dollar's worth. He had felt love for that horse the minute he had laid his eyes on her.

"Fourteen dollars and fifty cents, fourteen dollars and seventy-five cents, fourteen dollars and eighty-five cents, fourteen dollars and ninety-five cents," Tom counted out loud. "Rats! I'm five cents short!" Then he remembered the five cents Dad had given him when they went to town last month that he still had in his jacket pocket. He ran and got it. After he recounted the money and put it in a sack he had, he ran outside and gave it to Mr. Smith. Mr. Smith took it to the car, spilled the contents on the seat, and counted it.

Why do grown-ups have to be so sure of everything? thought Tom.

"It's all here," said Gary. "Let's unload the horse and put her in the barn."

Chapter 6
The Horse's New Home

After the horse was in the barn and Gary had left, Dad went to the attic of the house and looked through some boxes. "Ah, here it is," said Dad. "At last!" Out of a box, he pulled a brown currycomb that he had had for his horse when he was a kid. Mr. Johnson put it in his shirt and walked down to the barn. There was Tom, just as he expected, currying his horse with a comb.

"Whoa there, Son. You don't want to get too close to the hindquarters. You don't know what kind of treatment this horse has had. Don't use that comb on a horse. Use this," said Dad, producing the currycomb from his shirt.

"Oh, wow! Thanks a lot, Dad," said Tom. "You're the greatest!"

"I used to have a saddle for old Bess, remember? I bet it is in that pile over there." Dad pointed to an old stack of boxes, pieces of scrap wood and metal. In a flash, Tom was over there digging in the pile.

"It's here! It's here!" yelled Tom as he held the most beautiful saddle he had ever seen. "There's a bridle and halter, too!" screamed Tom, running over to the horse. "I'll have to name you. I'll name you Angel. Let's see how this saddle looks on you," he said, putting the saddle over the horse and fastening the strap underneath.

"Whoa, Son," said Dad. "You'd better take the horse out to the corral and let me ride her. We don't know how she handles."

As Tom led Angel to the corral, he thought about her and how much his mom would have liked her.

When Dad got on Angel, she didn't bolt or run. She just stood there. "Giddyup," said Dad, as he kicked Angel's ribs. Angel started in a trot and soon speeded up into a gallop as Dad steered her. "She handles well! I'll let you try her," he shouted.

When Dad pulled Angel to a stop, Tom ran up to her and climbed on. "Giddyup!" As he was riding around the corral, he thought about what he used to do with old Bess and decided to try it.

"Jump!" yelled Tom, pulling up on Angel's neck. At that command, the colt jumped over the fence and landed on the ground about ten feet outside the fence. "Giddyup!" yelled Tom, as the horse took off at high speed. After galloping about one hundred yards, Tom yelled, "Whoa!"

"I think you got more than you bargained for," exclaimed Dad.

Chapter 7
A Second Visitor

A week later, Tom and his dad were at the kitchen table eating breakfast when there was a knock on the door. Tom answered it. Mr. Davison, an old friend of the Johnsons, stood in the doorway. "Word's getting around town about your new horse," said Mr. Davison, sitting down. "I came here to tell you about a race the town is sponsoring. Everyone who has a horse can enter and the prize is five hundred dollars for first place, two hundred for second, and fifty for third. The race is Saturday at 2:30 P.M. If you decide to race, you need to be there at 10:00 A.M.—if you want to get a stall to keep your horse in. Oh, and they don't allow saddles, so practice riding bareback for a while. Well, so long. I've got to go. I promised my wife I'd fix the car." Then Mr. Davison got up and walked out the door.

I'm going to enter that race, vowed Tom silently.

Chapter 8
The Race

The following Saturday was sunny, the perfect day for a race. Tom and his dad had made arrangements for a neighbor, Gregory Sours, to come by and pick up Angel, Tom, and Mr. Johnson in his horse trailer, since he was going to town that day anyway.

Tom was excited as he ate his toast and eggs. He was wearing white shorts that came down to his knees and a white button shirt, with a plaid hat on his head just like he had seen on television. He had just finished his last piece of toast when he heard a truck pull up. He looked out the window and saw Mr. Sours' truck and horse trailer pulling into the yard. Tom could hardly believe it was already 9:30 A.M. and time to leave. He ran out the door and told Mr. Sours that Angel was in the barn. Soon Angel was loaded in the trailer with Tom sitting beside her. The two men got in the truck and they started the trip to town. On the way, Tom could feel the tension in the air.

The stalls were quiet when they got to the fairgrounds. They found a stall from which they could see the racetrack. Soon other horses started arriving. They all looked better and faster than Angel, but Tom still had confidence in her.

"First call for three-year-old horses," called out the loudspeaker.

"All right, Son, go show them who's boss!" said Dad, opening the stall door and leading Angel to the track.

Tom mounted. "On your marks!" the starter

yelled. "Get set!" The starter paused a moment, letting the tension build up. All was quiet, and then *BANG!* The crowd went wild.

Tom thought he had gotten a good start, but he wasn't so sure when he saw three men pass him on the first hundred yards; but then, without any urging, Angel speeded up, as if knowing the importance of the race. Tom felt better when he saw that he had passed a man and then another, but he still had the head man to beat, and he was a good fifty yards ahead. Tom saw the distance shorten and knew he had a chance. Angel and the other horse were on the homestretch when Angel pulled up neck and neck with the lead horse and then passed him. Tom and Angel were in the lead! They were flying down the homestretch! They were five feet ahead of the other horse when they crossed the finish line. Before Angel could stop, people were snapping pictures, slapping Tom on the back and congratulating him. As Dad lifted Tom off the horse, the mayor came over and shook Tom's hand. "That was a good race you ran," he said. "How did you feel when you passed Johnny Good on the homestretch?"

"I never doubted Angel or God for one minute," said Tom, shaking the mayor's hand and clutching the five-hundred-dollar check that was handed to him.

Chapter 9
The Problem

The next Saturday, Tom was sitting at the kitchen table struggling over the words in the weekly newspaper they had bought when they had gone to town the evening before. On the second page was a picture of a horse with the caption: "Boy wins horse race at county fairgrounds. For story, see SPORTS, page 14." Tom turned there and read the story. It said that Tom Johnson had won the race and gave all the details. Tom tore the article out of the newspaper and ran down to the barn to show Angel.

"That's you!" Tom said to Angel, showing her the picture. "That's you! You won the race. I love you," he said, kissing her on the nose.

At breakfast on Tuesday morning, Dad said, "Son, I've been meaning to talk to you. Ever since you won that race, you've been paying too much attention to that horse. You are not getting your chores done, and you are ignoring people. You used to do nice things for others, but now you are just doing things for yourself and Angel. Do you think God likes that?"

"No, sir," mumbled Tom.

Chapter 10
The Angel

Several days later, Tom went down to the barn and saddled Angel. They trotted together for about forty-five minutes through the hills. Tom saw the sun setting and knew it was time to go home. He turned Angel around and started galloping back home. They were almost home when Tom saw a blur go before his eyes and realized he was falling. As he hit the ground, Tom felt a sharp pain in his leg. He didn't feel the pain when he saw Angel lying on the ground a foot away. She was lying very still.

"Angel," Tom whispered. "Angel!" Tom yelled, tears in his voice.

As Tom limped home to get his father, he couldn't see well because the tears were blurring his eyes. He thought of all the good times he had had with Angel.

When Tom told his father about Angel, they walked up to where Angel was. "She's dead, all right. I don't know how. She probably tripped in a gopher hole and hit her head on a rock," said Dad, trying to hold back the tears.

Chapter 11
Mr. Smith Again

A day after Angel was put in a box and buried, there was a knock on the door. Tom answered it, and there stood Gary Smith. "Oh, hi, Mr. Smith. I guess you heard about Angel."

"Yes, I did. She was a good horse, wasn't she? I'm sorry about what happened," said Mr. Smith.

"Hello, Gary," said Dad, coming out of the living room. I'm glad you're here. There are some questions I've been wanting to ask you."

"Well, shoot," said Gary.

"For starters, why did you come up here to sell the horse. Why didn't you stay in Virginia?" questioned Dad.

"Well, Virginia is known for her horses, and most people have good horses there. I came where most people don't have horses."

"Did the horse have any training before you brought her here?"

"You bet she did! Her father was the great Chamád!"

"You mean the horse that won the Kentucky Derby five years in a row?"

"That's the one!"

"Why was Angel so skinny and ungroomed when she came here, and why did you sell her for such a small amount?" asked Tom.

"My father was a very giving man, and he gave Angel to a very sick child that wanted a horse. When the boy died, his parents neglected Angel and finally returned her to my father. Before Dad died, though, he wrote in his will that I must sell her to someone I knew would care for her if I were to inherit my portion. I knew you would when I saw you. Since I would be getting my money, the price did not matter."

Chapter 12
Tom's Thoughts

For many days after that, Tom couldn't get over not having Angel to ride and keep him company. But he knew deep down inside of his heart that God took Angel away from him for a good reason. Perhaps it was because he was spending so much time with her and not getting his chores done or because he was putting her first in his life and not God. But whatever the reason, Tom knew there would always be good things to remember: the race at the fairgrounds, Mr. Smith, the money he won. Most of all, though, Tom would remember the good times he had with Angel, his horse. She would live in his mind forever.

AWFUL DAY

by
Michiko Hanao

"This is a new student from Japan," said the teacher. "Your seat is over there."

This teacher is so strange. She didn't introduce my name! I thought, Weird teacher.

I came from Japan three days ago. Now I'm in school. I am so sleepy because of the time. It's confusing between Japan's time and America's time. They are opposite.

"What's your name?" asked someone.

I didn't know what she was saying so I shook my head. I wanted to go back to my house, so I could sleep in a big comfortable bed and see a dream that is no school every day. But I couldn't.

This classroom is soooo awful. People are giggling and another group is talking loudly. If this was Japan, the teacher would get angry. And there is one person who is strange. I think she has some kind of problem.

Fifteen minutes later, the bell rang. *Buzzzzzzzzzzzz.* Everyone went to their desk. First we had math. It was so easy. Just three-digit quotients. I don't know what the teacher is saying,

I thought to myself. On the blackboard it read: pgs. 102, 103, 104. I decided, I have to do pages 102, 103, and 104. Everyone was talking, laughing, and sharing the answers. In Japan, if anyone talked, laughed, or shared answers, the teacher would get angry.

Later that day, at 10:55 A.M., we heard "Help!" A person screamed from the back of the room. Everyone turned to look at her. It was the strange person who has a problem. I turned to look at her, too. Everyone opened their eyes real big.

"What happened?" asked the teacher.

"Th . . . the . . . an . . . ant! It's red, it's big, and it's on my desk!"

What is happening? I wondered.

"Just leave it alone," said the teacher.

"No, no, I hate ants!"

"Just leave it," the teacher said again.

The strange person ran away from her desk. Everyone laughed and laughed. I couldn't understand why. The person who was sitting next to the desk brushed the ant from the desk.

"OK, it's over," said the teacher.

"In Japan's schools, there wouldn't be any ants," I grumped.

Half an hour later, the teacher said, "It's lunch time."

Everyone walked to the closet. I walked there, too. Then I looked around to see what they were doing. They took out their lunches, so I did too.

We walked to the lunch room. There were about ten big tables. I sat on a chair and ate my sandwich. Everyone talked. Thirty minutes passed quickly. Then the bell rang, *Buzzzzzzz.*

We were back in our classroom. A few moments later my name was called. A few people were sitting at the reading table.

"Sit here," said the teacher. Then she patted the chair. I thought, I have to sit on the chair.

Then the teacher said, "Read this."

I was just looking at the book. Then suddenly everyone laughed. I didn't know why they were laughing.

"Next person read," said the teacher. The teacher was saying something to everyone.

What is she saying? I thought. And this book is too hard for me!

I didn't know the lesson was over but everyone closed their book. I thought it was over. Then the teacher handed me a workbook. But I thought to myself, I can't do this! I can't read!

"Take out your social studies book," said the teacher.

Then everyone took out the book that had a picture of a farm in it. So I looked inside the desk. Finally I found it. I opened the book. It looked like a dictionary because there were lots of words that I didn't know. Then the teacher wrote on the blackboard: Silently read to pg. 96.

"NO!" everyone screeched.

I couldn't figure out why they were saying that.

The classroom was so quiet. No sound. It was silent.

Why is it so quiet? I thought.

"Is everyone finished?" asked the teacher.

"NO!" a few people shouted.

"Ten more minutes and we will discuss the pages," said the teacher.

Ten minutes later, they were reading, taking turns. And sometimes the teacher was asking something.

Then the teacher gave out the tests.

What's this? I thought.

I didn't understand, so I wrote my name and returned the blank sheet of paper.

A little later, the teacher said, "Put away your social studies book and take out your homework pad."

Everyone was looking inside the desk.

"OK, write: Math, page 106 and Read science book to page 202," said the teacher. They all were writing.

"Bring your jackets and packs," said the teacher.

Everyone walked to the closet and suddenly everyone talked. Everyone got their stuff so I got mine, too. I put my pencil case in the pack. The pack was so light because I didn't know what to put in it.

Buzzzzzzzzzzzzzzzzzzzzzzz. The bell rang.

"'Bye! See you tomorrow," said the teacher.

Most awful day, I thought to myself. So different from Japan.

KATE DID IT

by
Eileen Markey

*We're no longer Little Children, no longer full
  of innocence.
Times, the times are gonna change. They
  never will be the same.
We're gonna grow a lot this year,
We're gonna change so much this year,
We're never gonna be the same,
Never gonna feel the same!
We're gonna face some problems. We're gonna
  learn to deal with them.
Times, the times are gonna change.
They're never gonna be the same.
We're gonna solve some mysteries,
We're gonna grow a lot this year,
We're never gonna be the same.
There's no turning back now,
The past has been torn out from beneath us.
  We've gotta step up now, we've gotta step
  together.
We're gonna learn about life,
We're gonna learn about death.
We're gonna laugh a lot this year,*

We're gonna cry a lot this year.
But we never will be the same, oh no!
Times, the times are gonna change indeed.
   They will never be the same. There's no
   turning back now, no way to stop time from
   going on. We'll learn to feel secure, now.
Times, the times are gonna change. They're
   never gonna be the same.
We've gotta just remember
We've got each other.

Kate wrote that. But we didn't find it until after.
Well, I guess I should start at the beginning.

Chapter 1
The Beginning

September 7th. The first day of school. Why was
I so nervous? Sixth grade can't be that bad, no
worse than fifth, or fourth, or third, or any school
grade, I guess. Then why was I so nervous? I have
an awesome class, great teachers, the safety patrol.
What could be better?

So, as shaky as a crisp fall leaf, I walked to sixth
grade, Mrs. Andersen's class, Room 14, to find all
my fears groundless.

The fifth-graders challenged us sixth-graders to
a soccer game two weeks into the year. I was invited to play by Michelle. I then saw a big plus
about sixth grade—the segregated groups, the
cliques, were starting to diminish, somewhat. The
game was super. Both boys and girls played. The
game was scheduled to start at 3:30 but it didn't
start until a quarter of four. Some people walked,

some rode their bikes. So there we were, shivering in the September breeze, with our pant cuffs rolled up and our collars up. Gossiping and freezing.

The reason everyone was so excited about this game is that the fifth-graders are real snobs. They're bossy and smug and horridly cliquey. They don't respect their elders in the least (we do), so we thought we'd take the challenge and teach them. Of course, *we* didn't want to challenge *them*. We're too nice a bunch and we didn't want to start a fight and lose our angelic image among the teachers. Well, finally the game started. In the begining it was orderly—eleven players per team, a coach for each team, substitutes, penalties and everything. But then we went haywire. We lost track of scores, and had to end the game when the field was needed for a practice.

The sixth-graders at the game were as follows: Michelle, myself, Andrea, Alison, Maureen, Colleen, Kate, Susan, Rachel, Joey, Mark, Teddy, Brian, Kevin, Pat, Shawn, and Eddy.

We had an awesome time even if everything did go crazy.

Chapter 2
Laughs and Funny Things

As the year progressed our class became known as the studious, quiet class. Of course, we were very funny too.

Our history teacher, Mrs. Basel, is very smart, and strict. One skill lesson in our book is "cause-and-effect" sentences. Mrs. Basel asked us to start a sentence and then the next person would say an effect. Joey started. He said, "He was playing with his pen . . ." Susan then said, ". . . and the pen exploded . . ." The sentence went on and on and had us, along with Mrs. Basel, laughing hysterically. We started a new sentence and it grew to concern pigs who were a snorting band! Joey, Mark, and Brian were the pigs. The pigs died and were then called the "Holy Snorters"! All the other classes must have wondered what was so amusing about a history lesson to have us laughing so hard we were crying!

Our fun continued. There was the "peripheral vision" episode, the "sweet Polly" episode and the "encompass" episode, for which I have not time, ink, or paper.

Chapter 3
And Fights, of Course

The girls' gym changing room was the battleground of words many times. Sometimes the fights were about the gym game scores. But most of the time they were about attitudes and personalities. Alison and Rachel often got into a fray with Colleen and Susan. Michelle and Maureen, Andrea and Alexis usually just kept quiet and shook their heads wondering, Why?

But it was Kate—the smart, bubbly, pretty, sentimental one—who was loved more than she knew. It was she who dangerously got in the middle and quieted the sides, tried to reason with them, and miraculously insured peace for the world of Room 14. Now you can see why Kate was so important to us all. She was a peacemaker and a friend. If anybody was feeling, lonely, sad, depressed, or, on the contrary, quite happy, Kate always was there. Every one of us loved her a wicked lot. Kate didn't think much of herself, though. I don't think she realized how much we loved her.

Chapter 4
Not Kate!

"Class, I have bad news," came Mrs. Andersen's voice, piercing the chatter. "The reason Kate's absent today is because she was hit by a car last night."

"Oh, no, not Kate!" breathed Andrea who was coming in the door. "Not Kate!"

"Yes," sighed Mrs. Andersen. "Last night at 5:30 on Roosevelt Avenue. A hit-and-run driver."

"Mrs. Anderson," asked Brian, "is it serious?" Yes, is it serious? the whole class's eyes seemed to say.

"I don't know," she told us. "Her leg is broken and her arm. I don't know if there are any internal injuries. They would be serious."

The entire class was on the verge of tears. No, not Kate! Mrs. Andersen explained that we would make cards for her. Susan immediately started to write a note to Michelle, her best friend. Susan's face was as pale as that of a ghost, unlike her usual rosiness which went with her red hair.

Dear Mich,
    What do you think about Kate? I can't believe she got hit! Oh my God!!!!!! What if she died? I'd kill myself for not having her over more often. We'll have

to go visit her today. We can bring a bunch of people. Do you know what hospital she's at? We have to go see her today. Maybe your sister can drive us.

I'll talk to you later.

Love,

Sue

Sue folded up the note ingeniously and had it passed to Michelle.

Shawn was writing a note to Joey.

Dear Speedy,

I can't believe Kate got hurt! I wonder who hit her? We should go see her today. All those broken bones. It sounds painful.

See you,

Shawn

Brian wrote Kevin this note:

Dear Kev,

Do you want to visit Kate today? We should get her some candies, or books. I wonder who the heck hit her. If she dies I'll never forgive myself for not talking to her more. I have to make the card.

From Brian

Alison wrote Rachel a note about all the times Kate had saved her from an all-out war with Susan and Colleen. Andrea wrote me a note; and as I watched her write it, I knew her tears were real, genuine tears, not the "artificial" ones she sheds so well.

The class had none of its usual spark that day.

After school two carloads full of unusually quiet children made their way to the hospital. When the classmates met in the lobby they went to the receptionist's desk to ask their friend's room number. The receptionist should have informed the children that no one under sixteen is allowed in that ward; but seeing the tender, caring look in the young faces, the kind woman directed them to Room 462.

The class stood silently in the elevator until they reached the fourth floor. The class walked numbly along through the hall with nothing in their minds but their dear friend Kate.

Chapter 5
Words of Wisdom

When Andrea led us into Room 462 we found Kate lying in the hospital bed writing something. In bed she seemed small, and her face was pale. Kate quickly put away her writings.

Our friend was in critical condition—a broken leg, arm, and back, along with internal injuries. Despite all this suffering, Kate smiled to see us.

Kate told us many things that afternoon. I'll try to repeat what she said to us:

"You guys are all awesome. You know that. I'm sure you pity me now, all these broken bones. I'll soon be released from all the pain. The doctors told me I'd die."

A general gasp followed by a sob filled the room.

"I guess that means you'll miss me. I'll miss you,

too, but listen carefully to what I want to tell you."

We were all ears. Through tear-filled eyes we looked at Kate, her blue eyes shining radiantly.

Kate went on. "You guys have to stop fighting. You fight too much. This year has been awesome; the cliques have melted a little and everyone's more friendly, but it's not enough. Alison and Rachel, you've gotta stop fighting with Sue and Colleen, and vice versa. I usually break up fights, but I can't do that anymore. Joey and Mark, you guys gotta stop leaving people out and calling them nerds. Kenny, Dave, and Frank, you guys gotta stop hatefully calling Joey and Mark 'preps.'" There was a pause as Kate closed her eyes and touched her side. Then she continued. "This whole class has gotta be more open, more loving. We, or you, can't have 'loners' or 'nerds' or 'geeks' or 'preps,' just friends. I know growing up is hard. I'm kinda glad I got out of it."

"No!" I said, but Kate just smiled at me.

"Seventh grade is gonna be tough. Mrs. Sloat and Mrs. Ace aren't easy teachers. You've gotta go in the seventh grade, and the rest of the grades *together*. When you think of doing something mean, just think of me and don't. I'll watch over you."

Kate stopped talking, but we didn't move. Then a nurse came in with medicine for her and said we had to leave. We started out the door.

"'Bye Kate," said Alison, speaking for all of us. "We'll see you soon."

Again Kate smiled.

Afterword

Kate didn't get better. The class went on together to seventh grade and many more grades. They often would start to argue or fight or form cliques, but they thought of Kate and stopped, and Kate smiled down on them like a sunbeam. Soon after she died Kate's will was read. She willed her earthly possessions to family members. To her class, however, she willed the poem which is on the first page. She also willed to the entire class her famous smile—and amazingly they all learned to use it, and it became a part of them.

THE WEIRDEST DREAM OF MY LIFE . . . PART III

by
Chris Joplin

In the last exciting and hilariously funny episode of "The Weirdest Dream of My Life," I awoke from what seemed to be a dream. It wasn't a dream, and I was three and a half inches tall.

So there I was—me, Chris Joplin, the size of a grasshopper.

LOOK OUT!

* close-up

The next week, my mom took me to the doctor at Burton Creek Medical Clinic, in downtown West Plains.

She walked to the receptionist's desk and set me on top of it.

"Yes, we have an appointment. The name? Sandra Joplin."

"If you'll wait just a moment, I'll . . . AYIEE!!!" *CLUNK!*

She had fainted. Not very good manners.

We went to the waiting room and waited . . . and waited . . . and waited . . . and waited, until . . .

"The doctor will see you now, Mrs. Joplin."

After my checkup, the doctor said, "Your son is in good health, except for one very small drawback. Ha, ha, ha! Funny, huh?"

I didn't laugh.

"Wait and see what happens. Come back next week."

After that, we went to Frederick's Pizza, and I ate a piece a whole inch in diameter. That's a lot, if you're three and a half inches tall.

On the way home, I accidentally left the window down, and I flew out like a gum wrapper!

Luckily, there was a bush to catch me, or I would have been the late Chris Joplin!

"Easy, Chris, don't lose your head!" I told myself.

I climbed down from the bush and studied my surroundings. It wouldn't have been so terrifying if I was normal in size, but to a person the size of a grasshopper, one- and two-story buildings look like the Empire State Building! I was surrounded by them!

I started walking on the sidewalk, jumping over the gaping cracks only a few centimeters wide.

"AYIEEE!!" I screeched. I had forgotten about all the people that walk on sidewalks. Fortunately, I didn't see the crack ahead of me, and I fell in it and was saved from looking like a deformed pancake.

I climbed out of the crack close to the side so I wouldn't get flattened. I walked and walked, and walked, and walked, and finally was out of the square. My brain kept trying to tell me that I was forgetting something, but it was already too late before I realized that I had passed my dad's office. I decided against kicking myself. It would probably slow me down.

It seemed as though I had been walking forever, but it was only five blocks.

Now it was dark, except for the streetlights. I decided to call it a day and sleep. I could have climbed up a tree or hid in a bush, but noooo! I had to be dumb and sleep right out in the open!

I was exhausted and dozed off in five minutes.

About three hours later, I was awakened by a horrifying sound: a dog's bark. It was coming closer.

When he noticed me, I did just about the dumbest thing I could have. I stood there, frozen to the ground, saying, "Nice doggie."

Then the dog walked up, began wagging his tail, and started licking me! I nearly drowned! I lost my temper and clobbered him on the nose.

"YIPE!" he bawled, and ran away. At that I resolved that it was too dangerous to sleep in plain sight and began walking, not stopping until the early morning.

"Whew! I can't take much more of this," I said,

after walking five blocks. "I've got to find some place to rest or I'll collapse!"

An enormous-looking bush looked comfortable, so I climbed up and fell asleep instantly, invisible to everyone.

When I woke up, I had a little trouble figuring out where I was.

"Omigosh! How did I get stuck in this tree? Wait a minute . . . Maybe if I knock myself upside the head, it'll give me an idea of what's going on."

WHACK!

"Now it's all coming back to me . . . and I'd better start walking if I'm going to be home by Christmas!"

So I started off walking, careful not to get run over by the cars.

WARNING:
IF YOU EVER HAPPEN TO SHRINK TO THREE AND A HALF INCHES TALL, DON'T TRY CROSSING THE STREET. IT COULD BE HAZARDOUS TO YOUR HEALTH.

I crossed street after never-ending street and dodged car after humongous car.

"Chris, you'd better find us some food down here, or we'll go on strike!" said my insides. I hadn't thought of this!

I looked around and noticed that the place looked strangely familiar. I was in my own neighborhood, a mile or two away from home and food!

"YIPPEE!" I rejoiced.

"It's about time," my insides said. It was then that I noticed a strange furry creature about the size of King Kong bounding gracefully toward me.

The creature, which was really a normal cat, stopped in front of me. I looked at it closely and realized that it was my very own cat, roaming around the neighborhood!

So I climbed up on her back and we began walking. Suddenly a dog appeared out of nowhere.

"No! Please . . . Anything but that!"

She had chased the dog many times, but not when I was riding her! I had nothing to hang on to but fur!

The cat chased the dog around the block; all around the neighborhood, never stopping. I somehow managed to stay on, saying my prayers silently. Luckily, she stopped right in front of our house and walked up the driveway. I jumped off and said, "Great. Nobody's home and I'll probably spend the rest of my entire life trying to get into my own house!"

Just then, I saw that my bedroom window was open. What good fortune! I heard a crash when I climbed in. What bad fortune. There seemed to be someone of the burglar persuasion in my house. I had come home at the wrong time and was about to faint. "Steady yourself, Chris," I told myself. "If you have to scream, scream quietly!" I opened my mouth.

"AYIEEEEEE!!!!!!!"

Then, the idea of the century came to me. "Of course! It's simple! All I have to do is tie clear fishing line from one wall to the other and wait for him to come out!"

So I did that and hid out of sight.

*ME TYING FISHING LINE TO WALL

The burglar stuck his head around the corner to see if the coast was clear.

Of course, he couldn't see the clear fishing line. He bolted down the hallway for the door but the string did its job.

—WHOA!

He toppled over and banged his head on the wall. He was out cold.

Now I only hoped my parents would get home before he woke up. Just then, another brilliant idea came to me. So far, every person who saw me in this condition had fainted, and maybe this guy would, too. I heard a groan from the hall and raced out there.

"Wha . . .?" he said in a slurred voice. Then he looked around and noticed me standing there.

Clunk! went his head as it hit the floor.

I heard the door open and Mom and Dad came in.

"Hey, Mom! Dad! Guess what? When I got home, the window was open and I climbed in and . . . Hey, you're not listening to me!" I had forgotten to yell and, therefore, they didn't even know I was standing in front of them! So I yelled them the whole story.

The police arrived and the criminal was apprehended, still knocked out cold. They had to carry him out to the police car.

That night, to celebrate my getting home and catching the crook, we ordered Frederick's pizza. This time, I ate a piece a whole two inches in diameter!

BROTHERLY LOVE

by

J. S. Eldridge

My name is Justin Eldridge and, let me tell you, if you think adopting a baby is easy, you're wrong! Adopting a baby is three million times as hard as cleaning your room! And that's a fact, but the results are beautiful! This story is about the results of an adoption.

It all started when my mom got us (my family) hooked up with an adoption consultant. Her name was Terry, and her job is to pick out birth mothers for certain families (a birth mother is someone who is putting her baby up for adoption).

Terry introduced us to Sussane, who was a birth mother. Sussane was seventeen and already had a fifteen-month-old girl. They both were living in a foster home.

The day had come that we were going to meet Sussane at the park. We spent the afternoon there with Sussane and Danielle, Sussane's daughter. While the adults talked, my sister, Cori, and I played in the play area. We left at about one o'clock, and had a regular Saturday.

After that meeting, Sussane had a choice to

make—if she was going to give the baby to us or to another family that wanted the baby too.

Some good news started to come our way in the month of September. Sussane had chosen us to get her baby! Our whole family was so overjoyed, we were practically bouncing off the walls!

After a while we calmed down and took Sussane and Danielle out a couple more times. Mom went shopping with Sussane. My family went out to dinner with her. We went to a lot more places with her, too.

In October, Sussane went in for a checkup at the doctor's and the doctor said that the baby would be born some time around Christmas, which to us was a long time!

Well, Christmas finally came but no baby! Christmas was lots of fun, but it would have been more fun with the baby!

On December 29, the family went out to do some shopping. When we came home I noticed something: Dad went straight to the answering machine (usually he takes his time).

That night, about 10:15, I heard Mom talking on the telephone. But she was using the tone of voice that she uses to talk with business people. I jumped out of bed and hid behind the couch to listen. Many thoughts went through my head, but they stopped when my mom hung up.

Then Mom picked the telephone up again. When she started to talk she didn't use her business voice, just her regular voice. Then I heard her say something about "it" and something about Sussane. Then Mom said, "It's a boy!"

I jumped out from behind the couch laughing

and dancing around. I also was so happy that I cried! Mom hung up the telephone and told me all about it. But she couldn't tell me much because the hospital couldn't tell us anything without permission from Sussane since she's the birth mother.

Mom did tell me that it was a boy and that we were going to call him Jered Stephen Eldridge. Mom also said that Dad and she were going to see and feed Jered that afternoon!

Mom called the hospital back and got more information about Jered. They said he weighed nine pounds, two ounces, and was twenty-one inches long. He was born at 10:15 at night, and he was in good shape!

That afternoon Mom and Dad went to see Jered, and got back at about two o'clock. Mom said that I could go and see him at four o'clock.

It was about 3:30. We took off for the hospital. When we got there I really didn't feel excited; but as we got closer to the nursery, my heart started to beat faster and faster.

Before we went in where the babies were, we had to wash up and put on these apron-like things. The first time I looked at Jered I thought he looked sort of ugly. But when I looked at him better, he looked beautiful! Mom got to hold him first, because she was going to feed him. But after that I got to hold him!

I got to hold him for about six minutes. Then Dad held him. I asked Mom if I could feed him, but she said Jered didn't know how to suck very well, and he could choke easily.

We stayed about an hour, then went to eat. When

we got home Dad went to bed because he had to go to work at 1:00 A.M. Mom and I stayed up until 10:30. But I didn't get to sleep until about eleven o'clock, because we were going to pick up Jered the next morning at 11:00. I was so excited!

We went to pick up Jered at 11:30. When we got to the hospital, we dressed Jered up. While Mom was doing that, Dad was signing adoption papers.

We carried Jered out to the car, and I got to sit by Jered on the way home. That day was so much fun! I got to hold Jered a million times!

That night was New Year's Eve, and we all went to a watch party, but Jered slept all through it.

The next day we went to pick up Cori, my sister, from Reno (she was spending some time with her cousin).

After we picked Cori up, we went to show one of our aunts and uncles the baby. We stayed about an hour and a half, then left.

A couple days later we went to our grandma's to spend a little time there. While we were there I got to change Jered for the first time!

Another couple of days flew by, and on one of those days I asked Mom if I could feed Jered, and she said yes!

Having a baby brother is lots of fun. The love that holds us together is very strong, and nothing can break it!

THE TALKING IGUANA

by
Andrew Eric Harrison

Chapter I

Lizard woke up early because he had to do his paper route. He is called Lizard because he has a humongous collection of pet lizards. He delivers papers because he wants to earn money to buy the iguana in the pet store.

Lizard does things very weirdly. He is as weird as Dr. Jekyll and Mr. Hyde. People say he shouldn't be a paperboy because he likes to put lizards in the papers. Once he threw a bouncie ball off the Empire State Building and it never came back up. He certainly is not a normal boy!

He got on his lizard-shaped bike, the U.S. Chameleon, and started off on his paper route with a lizard in each paper.

As he was coming down the road, a car almost hit him. He lost control of his bike on the bike jump and went flying into the Lost Woods.

Lizard's bike landed in a tree and he fell into a creek. Then he said, "My bike's luckier than I am!"

Lizard was lost, and he walked into the woods

until he found an old cabin. Inside there was a wise old man who had a short white beard and was wearing pink polka-dot pants and no shoes.

Lizard was frightened but the gentle old man told Lizard not to be afraid. He had planned for Lizard to end up at the cabin.

The old man said he would grant Lizard two wishes. Lizard was excited and couldn't decide.

His first wish was he wanted to go home because he missed his family.

His second wish was for a talking iguana.

Chapter II

Before he knew it, he was back in his own bedroom with a green, three-foot-high iguana next to him. Lizard was staring at the iguana in amazement when the iguana said, "What are you looking at?" Lizard was shocked and knew his wish had come true.

Lizard gave the iguana a skateboard and they both rode over to Frog Legs' house. Frog Legs is Lizard's best friend. He is called Frog Legs because that is his favorite food.

As soon as Frog Legs saw the iguana he said, "What the heck is that thing?" Then the iguana said, "Well, you certainly show respect!" "It is the talking iguana that I wished for," said Lizard. Frog Legs got very excited and said, "What should we name him?" Then Lizard said, "How about Iggie, which is short for iguana?" "Okay," said Frog Legs.

Now Lizard had to think of a way to tell his parents about Iggie.

Chapter III

Now Lizard was very smart. He bought a collar and a leash at the pet store, put them on Iggie, and told him not to talk—NO MATTER WHAT!

As soon as he got home, he dragged Iggie up to his room and told him to hide under his bed. Lizard's mom, Mrs. Turner, called up the stairs that it was time for piano lessons with his teacher, Miss Frump. Lizard told Iggie to stay put, and then he went downstairs. Iggie came downstairs anyway, snuck up behind Miss Frump and said, "What a fat frump you are!" Miss Frump turned to Lizard and said, "What did you say?" Lizard didn't say anything but Iggie repeated it. Miss Frump was furious. She got up and told Mrs. Turner she would never come to their house again because Lizard was rude. Lizard was in trouble! He was sent to his room and was not allowed to play for two days.

While Lizard was sulking in his room, Iggie searched for a phone and placed a thousand-dollar bet on a show horse. He used Lizard's dad's name, Fred Turner. Lizard knew he could no longer have a talking iguana.

Chapter IV

Lizard was sitting alone in his room wondering what was going to happen next. He was very sad because he was being punished for things he didn't do. Then he said out loud, "I wish I never had a talking iguana."

Suddenly the old man appeared and asked if he

wanted to give away his wish. He said yes right away. In an instant Iggie was gone. The old man then said he would give Lizard's wish to someone else.

Somewhere in the neighborhood someone screamed.

DAYS ON THE BUS

by
Ron Riske, Jr.

It is not fun to ride the school bus every day. When you first start it is fun, and you want to ride every day for the rest of your life. You get to see the countryside and you feel high in command. But after a while it is boring, and you think you are going to ride forever. The seats get very hot when you wear shorts in the summer and you're sitting on plastic. When you see the same thing every day it gets downright boring. When you put your head on the window in the summer it gets very hot. You try every lie that yo-yos use. You try every excuse in the book to keep from riding the bus. You begin to think that you can jump off the bus, and what other interesting transportation could you get home. When you start to get on the bus you start to think, I can run away from this place. Believe me, I have my share of lies to keep from riding: One is that you can't find your notebook and you can't go without it. Another is: Your shoe is missing. The day's end is horrible. The bus driver yells at the teenagers for putting their feet on the seat. She yells at me for eating on the bus.

The city people don't know what it's like. They just don't know what it's like.

THE FARMER'S CHOICE

by
Johnny Quiñones

It was a cold November night and in just a few days it was going to be Thanksgiving. The farmer and his wife couldn't make up their mind whether to eat turkey, chicken, or duck. Their son would be coming down for Thanksgiving from college.

The next day the farmer went to see the turkey, the chicken, and the duck. "Lets see, which one is the plumpest?" said the farmer.

"The turkey is," said the chicken.

"No, I'm not," said the turkey.

Then the chicken said, "If you're going to kill me, who is going to make your eggs?"

"You know, you're right," said the farmer.

"You can't eat me because I'm weak and lean. You want somebody like the duck," said the turkey.

"Who are you talking to?" said the wife.

"Nobody," said the farmer.

"Well, if you kill me, who's going to crow for you?" said the turkey.

"But I thought that was the rooster's job," said the farmer.

"It is, but I'm getting better at it and it isn't the thought that counts it's the crow," said the turkey.

"If you kill me, you're not really going to have a real farm," said the duck.

"Every farm has a chicken, duck, and turkey," said the turkey.

"Now don't you want to keep that good reputation for having the best farm?" said the chicken.

"Why don't you go kill Mr. Cow, Mr. Pig, or Mr. Billy Goat?" said the chicken.

The farmer went away to think about it.

Then came that big day, Thanksgiving.

"Who are you going to kill?" said the chicken.

"Well, I'm going to kill the turkey, duck, and chicken," said the farmer, and he did.

After the feast, the farmer thought he had made a good choice. The next day he went to get a new chicken, duck, and turkey.

"Next Thanksgiving we'll have the same thing," said the farmer.

My Fishy Friends

by
J. J. Donohue

Hi, my name's Peter. I live in London with my grandfather. I am ten and have a lot of freckles.

My best friend's name is Billy. He lives right down the lane from me. Every day after school we go fishing. He always calls me, so I rush home and wait for him to call.

When we go fishing, Billy brings his fish home. I throw mine back. I wonder what he does with all those fish? Does he play ball with them instead of . . . ME? Does he have sleepovers with them instead of . . . ME? I had to find out if fish could play.

The next day I brought home all the fish I could carry. I rushed upstairs, shut the door, got out my Scrabble game, and TRIED to play with the fish. It was obvious they didn't know how to play. So I told them some of my best jokes. They didn't laugh at one! They just lay there looking exhausted.

"I was a fool to believe my best friend would play with dumb fish instead of me," I said in a loud whisper.

"I resent that remark," said a pudgy fish that had suddenly come to life.

"I-I-I'm ssssorry. I didn't know—oooooo, wait a second! CAN you really play?" I said slyly.

"Hey, boys," the fish said to all the others. "This here boy wants to know if we can play." They all giggled and then said, "Can we play? We can play better than you and your fifteen best friends. Want to see?"

And before I could answer, all the fish were running, jumping, and doing cartwheels all over my room. Soon they were all laughing out of glee, and before I noticed it, I was laughing too.

"You guys really can play better than me and fifteen of my best friends," I said in pure delight.

"If you think we play good in your small room, you should see what we could do at home," said a fish with a top hat who was juggling three balls.

"Well, can I come with you to the lake, just for a little while?" I asked hopefully.

"Sure, you can stay as long as you want because while you're gone, time will be stopped," said the same fish, only now he was balancing all three balls on his scaley nose.

"All right I'll come," I decided, and with that I was under water at the bottom of the lake. The weird thing was, I was dressed totally different. Instead of jeans, I was wearing bright green shorts and a shirt with cut-off sleeves, also green. My shoes were green with white stripes through them.

I was taken through a narrow passage with walls of seaweed. Soon I was in a huge auditorium filled with everything a boy or fish could want—jungle gyms, swing sets, and lots of fun things like that.

My heart raced as I ran to the equipment. As soon as I sat on the swing the whole room filled up with little guppies.

I was laughing and playing and having the best of times, when I heard a clock strike 3:00 A.M. I ran, or actually swam, over to the fish who had been juggling in my room and said, "I thought you said time would be stopped while I was down here."

"I know, I know," cried the fish. "But it's the rule that when the first human comes down here, he or she must stay. However, I know a way out. You have to get to the surface before 3:30 A.M. I'll go with you; but we'll have to sneak, for if we are seen by any other fish I will be arrested and you will have to stay forever."

Soon we were tiptoeing and tipfinning through the seaweed hall and weren't seen by any fish. I checked my watch; only six minutes left. I was climbing a long stairway with the fish when we were stopped! An alarm was set off, and the chase was on!

I climbed those stairs like my feet were on fire! Not far behind I could hear the slapping of fins on the stairway, coming faster and faster.

Just as a scaley fin reached out and brushed my feet, I was at the surface. I swam to shore as fast as I could. With my first step on shore, my old clothes were on me and I was perfectly dry. I ran home and as soon as my head touched the pillow, I was asleep. I was awakened by the sweet smell of pan-

cakes. I walked wearily down the stairs. As soon as I was done eating, I called Billy.

When he answered he said something I didn't expect to hear. He said, "H-H-H-Hello?" and I asked, "Billy, can you play?" And here's the scary part:

He said, "Pete, I know you won't believe this, but I'm gonna stay home and play with some fish."

GROWING UP

by
Naomi Anne Schaefer

Dedicated to my Grandma
who encouraged me to write this story

1 Introduction

Trying to think of one word to define the phrase "growing up" could be impossible. Laughter, tears, smiles, and friendship are all parts of this sometimes wonderful thing.

My name is Naomi. Growing up is what I am trying to do now. It takes patience, understanding, and a lot of courage.

Sometimes I wonder how other children of my age do it.

I try to think of this as a phase every kid ten years or older goes through. I try not to think that I'm the only one who has this many troubles with it.

Every time I turn around, things get more difficult. Finding someone who will always understand what I would like to talk about isn't easy either.

Sometimes it's just best to talk to yourself or even a doll. Either way they can't talk back to you. Sometimes I just need advice so I go talk to someone, anyone who remembers what it's like to be ten.

2 Brothers and Sisters

Do you have a little shadow trailing you when you walk? If you do, you must have a younger brother or sister.

They can be problems, and having them around is troublesome when you have your own problems to deal with.

Personally I think it's best not to be fooled by how sweet they can be because next thing you know they'll be coming back to bug you again. Of course, it is nice to have someone who looks up to you. But that means you have to set a good example for someone, and that can be hard to do.

Younger brothers and sisters tend to be "snoopers." You must "lock your room and swallow the key."

They might be dangerous too. When little brothers and sisters are mad, they can get wild.

My suggestion is if they do get violent once, ignore it. If they do it again, cry, even if it does not hurt. This will attract your parents' attention. If they see you are crying and your brother or sister is not, they will feel sorry for you.

But after all this, younger sisters and brothers are really lovable and they are great company. You should really try to recognize the good qualities deep inside them.

3 Friendship

If you have been wondering what the true meaning of friendship is, well, I just found out.

Togetherness. If you and your friend share this, you are true friends forever.

Friends can always have disagreements, but if you don't apologize, you're not true friends anymore.

Even if after an argument your friend acts nice, you can bet he will probably start another argument.

If you apologize first, don't feel like you chickened out. It takes a lot of courage to do that. Don't try to wait for your friend to apologize. Remember your friendship is at risk.

True friends are with you no matter what you look like, how you feel, or how popular you are.

You might be better off if you had a few things in common with your friend but it does not make a big difference. Most of all, a friend is someone you can trust.

4 Popularity

Popularity is something you gain by your looks and who your friends are. It is not something important, but I suppose it depends on your point of view.

The negative side of popularity is the fact that, if you decide to be a friend with an unpopular person, you immediately become unpopular. This means you can never be different.

The positive side is you will always have friends.

They might not be "true friends," but they count for something.

You just have to hope you never become fat and you always keep up with fads.

Before you try to become popular, warn your family. They may have to associate with your friends' parents and brothers and sisters for the benefit of your popularity.

5 Fathers

Bad jokes, sarcastic comments, and ghosts in the kitchen at midnight. If you have these symptoms you have a father.

Fathers really do try their hardest, but everyone has a complaint.

Fathers are very active, fun, and understanding. They can always be helpful. If you have too many complaints about your father, talk to him. It helped me.

Sometimes they don't understand your point of view in some situations. In other situations, fathers laugh at something you consider serious. Fathers have personalities all their own. No other person seems like a father.

I think of a father as a privilege to have.

But if you want privileges, you must take on responsibilities along with them.

So treat your father with loving care.

6 Mothers

Here are some amazing people: mothers. They can explain a lot to you.

They can be very stern and strict, but personally I think you should ignore things like punishments. If your mother finds that they don't annoy you, she will stop giving them.

You can talk to mothers about almost anything. When you converse you will find them understanding and helpful.

A lot of mothers have hot tempers, not only with children but with other adults. You can't help but love them, though, with all the things they do for you, from tucking you in at night to waking you up in the morning.

All mothers are different. Some are fashionable. Some don't even know what the word means. Some try to be fashionable but don't succeed. This is where relatives come in!

7 Grandparents

Although most of the time grandparents take your parents' side, on certain occasions they feel sorry for you. They love your ideas and suggest that you build on them.

They bring you presents as if to say, "I hope these make up for lost time." Well, sometimes it does and sometimes it doesn't, depending on the present.

Sometimes you envy grandparents. After all, they're retired and have no homework. In other words, they're free. But sometimes you don't envy them. They don't run as much, play as much, and sometimes they're lonely without their sons and daughters who bring laughter into their lives. You can talk to them about almost anything: problems at school, at home, away, and with certain people.

You may think they don't understand your point of view, but they were probably just like you when they were kids at age ten.

8 Teachers

Long projects, a lot of homework, and writing on a blackboard. If you have these symptoms you have a teacher.

A teacher can be very sensitive. If she tells you she learned how to be the way she is from her teacher, you'd think she'd feel sympathetic to your problem, especially if she had already been through it.

There is another view—that the teacher feels this is what she has been waiting for. After all, if her teacher got to do "it" to her, shouldn't she get to do "it" to you?

This "it" I'm writing about, well you probably know this already but I'll explain anyway.

Some teachers are overly superior. One wrong move and you could be in the principal's office copying down 100 times, "I will not interrupt the class." (Or will I?)

Teachers understand a lot about you, but sometimes you don't feel like they know enough to give you advice.

9 Talk to Yourself

Before you shout out all your feelings after a fight, think about this. When you shout out all your feelings, people will know you're mad and try to annoy you more.

Instead of getting into trouble by shouting mean things to people, you should talk to yourself. Say whatever you want in your head without getting into trouble, because no one can read your mind and punish you for something they can't prove you did.

Talking to yourself helps you to calm down and let your feelings out. If you think you're right and somebody else is wrong, just tell this to yourself over and over. Doing this will give you the courage and confidence to talk out loud about what is bothering you. If you do this enough, you can tell the entire world.

10 Fads

You're in or out. Which is it going to be? This is a hard decision.

Here are some facts you should know before you automatically say "in." If you're going to be "in," remember you're basing every friendship you ever had on fads. One slip and you're going to be miserable. For instance, one day you go to your friend's house for a party. You make a mistake and you wear a pair of earrings from last month's fad. You're sunk. Your "in" friends will throw you "out," but your true friends, if you still have any after making your decision, will come to the rescue as usual. If you stay "out," who knows? You may start a fad all over the country. (Besides, fads are just not sensible.)

11 Being Sensible

Is it sensible? If not, what is it? Sometimes you just don't care. You want it and you won't give up until you get it.

You go to your friend's house; he has a new toy you can't live without. You come home, take a deep breath, and say, "I want it! I want it! I want it!" Sometimes you get it, and sometimes you don't.

Is it going to help you learn, is it going to make you generous, or is it just there to pass the time?

Before you say "I want it," think of a good reason for getting it, like, "This will entertain me all day so I won't bother you when you work." Explain and highlight the positive points but don't mention the negative points.

12 Comparison

Sometimes you may wonder about how much different you are at school and at home. Well, at school you want to act like a regular kid, up on fads and fashions. You want to act grown up. You want to fit in. You want to act "cool" in front of your friends.

On the other hand, at home you don't care because your friends can't see you. They can't tell you about your clothes or the way you act. You're around people you're really comfortable with. However, depending on who you are and who your friends are, you will probably feel comfortable having your true friends over to your house. After all, they like you for what you are, not for what you have, what you wear, or even how you act sometimes.

13 Being Bright Isn't Always a Delight

When you're smart, a lot of people just think you were born that way. In some cases this may be true but in most it isn't.

Some say that you have responsibility when you're smart. Most people, lazy or otherwise, don't like a lot of responsibility. Being responsible means striving for good grades, making careful decisions, and having respectful opinions. It's not easy to be responsible. However, many adults say that you should be glad you have this talent.

It really depends on how you think about it. You may think about it as another weight to carry on your shoulders or you may think of it as a special characteristic that separates you from the rest of the world. Well, right now it may not be as important as your popularity and other things like that, but grownups always tell you it will help you in the long run.

14 Conclusion

Everything that is written here I have discovered by myself. I have had all these problems and I have come up with these solutions.

Growing up is one of the hardest things to do in life. It definitely has the most challenges.

When you're a kid you want to be grown up, but when you're an adult, you'll most likely want to be a kid again. There's no way to avoid growing up, no matter *what you do*.

Since growing up is unavoidable, perhaps the best approach is to accept the challenge. Set goals for yourself. They could be daily or yearly. Then you'll know if you've accomplished new things and if you've really grown.

All this advice is just fine and dandy. But I often wish I didn't have to grow up!

MY TRIP TO SCHOOL

by
Mario Demasi

Chapter 1
Up, Up and Away?

I woke up one morning. I looked at my bright red digital clock and it said 8:45. I thought it said 5:45 because I was hardly awake, and slept for another two hours! It was now 10:45 and I realized I had to go to school.

Finally at ten till eleven I got up. I got out the milk container. Noticing it was empty, I got out the orange juice container and poured myself a very, very little glass of juice. I brushed my teeth and took a shower and realized that I missed the bus and my parents already went to work.

Chapter 2
The Walk

I got outside and it was freezing. All I had on was a light jacket. Oh well. I had to walk four miles so I had to get started.

It seemed like every car that went by splashed

me with either water or mud. I almost got run over by a city bus, and seven black cats crossed my path. I was only half the way there! I was hoping the other half would be better but it wasn't. It was worse, much worse.

Chapter 3
The Other Half

I had about two miles to go. It was fine getting there until three more black cats crossed right in front of me, and sixteen people asked me if I was lost. One of them told the police that a child was lost and they described me.

I had to go to the police station and tell them I was late for school and had to walk. They said "OK," and let me go.

Still two miles to go, since I'd had to walk backward toward the police station. I had to cross the street. Nothing was coming so I stepped out into the street. All of a sudden a van pulled out from an alley and almost hit me! When I jumped back I fell down. I had to go to the hospital.

Chapter 4
X-rays

I was at the hospital and they were taking X-rays. They told me I was OK but they had to take at least five more X-rays. It was now ten till one.

I didn't know if I was going to make it and I thought I was going to die.

Still two miles to go since the hospital was way back. Finally I could get started.

I walked one mile but still had one to go. I was wondering if anything would happen to me but nothing did.

Chapter 5
Three Down, One to Go

One more mile to go. I was walking and nothing had happened to me so far.

I thought I was close to school but I wasn't. I still had three-fourths of the mile to go. It was already 1:20!

I thought, Nothing has happened to me so far. Boy I wish I could get to school.

I kept walking. School was out at 2:30. I had to walk fast. Only one-fourth of the mile to go. It was 1:30.

I saw it! School! I was there! Still forty-five minutes of school. I had to hurry.

Chapter 6
Day of the Week

I ran. If I didn't get to school I'd be in big trouble. I got to the big double doors. They were locked. I shook them and knocked. I couldn't get in.

Then I remembered. I looked at my calendar watch. It was Saturday.

A WINTERY DAY

by

Luci Crawford

On school days,
Waiting for the little old bus,
I look at the driveway.
It looks like a sandwich
Made of rock, ice, and snow.

I look at the start of the fields.
The fences are encased with ice.

Down at the end of the field,
A little creek that was frozen
Has tiny streams trickling through the thick ice.

Semis go by.
They make the snow look like fireworks
That land on the trees.

The tree branches appear to me
Like drooping drapes,
Hanging almost to the ground.

Wherever ice falls,
It makes designs in the snow.

And as the sky goes dark,
The night grows still.
Then there is nothing left to see
Except a little banana moon
Glued on a black piece of paper.

THEY CALLED IT DARE MOUNTAIN

by
Amanda J. Sullivan

Chapter 1
Dare Mountain

The people in the town called it "Dare Mountain." Nobody had ever climbed it and made it back alive. Fourteen-year-old Kirk Stinley knew a boy, Kenny, whose father had tried to climb it, but he was never seen again.

It was June 24. Soon it would be the fourth of July and the big parade would go marching by. Kirk was thinking about the parade when all of a sudden the phone rang.

"Hello?" said Kirk. "Crazy Kirk's Cavern, may I help you?" He was in a crazy mood today.

"Hi, Kirk? This is Michael. Hurry! Turn on the TV. Channel 8. Watch the news. Call me back later."

"Why?" *Click.*

"Hey, Mike, come on!" But Michael had hung up the phone.

Kirk hung up. He ran to the living room, hopping over some of his baby sister's toys. He turned on the TV.

"Welcome to Channel 8 News. Tonight we have an interesting issue about what the townspeople call 'Dare Mountain.' Will there ever be a real name for it? We'll be back after these messages."

"KIRK! Come here a minute, please!"

"Oh, Mom, I'm watching the news!"

"Now, Kirk! I need help."

"Oh! Mothers! They never understand," he mumbled, climbing the stairs.

"What's that, Kirk?"

"Nothing!" He finished climbing the stairs. There he saw his mother with a bandana around her head. She was trying to lift up a big oak table. "Kirk, you wanna help me, please?"

"Sure. Where's Dad?"

"He's at work. He's got a new case."

"Oh brother! Now he'll be talking about it all the time. B-O-R-I-N-G!" Kirk sang out.

"Now, Kirk, that was not very nice! You know how much your father loves his work. Now I won't tell him about it this time, but next time . . . well, you just keep your mouth shut. Okay?" she said. "Now help me move this table, please."

"Yeah. Sure." They moved the heavy oak table and put it in the corner. Then Kirk ran down to the living room and sat down on his favorite cushioned chair. This he called "his" chair. The news came on.

"And that exciting adventure on Dare Mountain sure was interesting. Now we have an exciting story about the—"

Kirk slammed the TV off. "DARN!" He yelled out loud.

"What's wrong, honey?"

"Nothing. Mom, can I call Michael, please?"

"Go ahead, but no more than fifteen minutes. Got that, darling?"

"Okay. Thanks." He walked over to the phone. He dialed Michael's number.

"Hello?" said the voice on the end of the line.

"Hi. Is Michael home?" asked Kirk.

"Hold on, Kirky," said Maria, Michael's 12-year-old sister. She joked around with Kirk a lot.

"Hey, Kirk! What's up? How'd you like that news special? Did you watch it? That sure was something!" Michael said, all in one big breath.

"Mikey, slow down! No, I couldn't watch the news. How was it?"

"You didn't watch it! I called you and I told you! Why didn't you?"

"I had to help my mom with a table. Sorry," Kirk said.

"It's all right. Jesse watched and taped it. Kenny couldn't watch it either, so we'll all get together tomorrow. Okay?" Michael asked.

"Yeah, sure. Michael, I have to hang up. I've got fifteen minutes to make all my phone calls. I have to call Jesse and Kenny."

"All right. Talk to ya later. 'Bye!"

"'Bye." Kirk hung up the phone. He dialed Jesse's number. "Hi. Is Jesse there?" he asked when Jesse's mom answered.

"Hold the line, please," Jesse's mother said. She was a secretary and talked like you wouldn't believe!

"Hello?" Jesse said.

"Hi, Jess! What's up?"

"Nothing much. My dad's being a real jerk. He taped Police Academy 3 over the Dare Mountain tape! Now how are you and Kenny supposed to watch it? The jerk."

"No way! How could your dad be so numbheaded?" Kirk replied, surprised.

"Of course, *he* could be that stupid. He's my dad!" yelled Jesse.

"Okay, okay! Sorry."

"Yeah, right. Hey look, Kirk, I can't talk now. I gotta go help my mom."

"Okay. See you later," said Kirk.

"Kirk, get off the phone now, please. I'm getting an important phone call," his mother said.

"Mom, can't I call Kenny? Puh-lease?" asked Kirk.

"I said no. I meant no. Now put on the answering machine and let's go. We have to pick your dad up."

"Oh!" Kirk grumbled.

When the station wagon pulled up to John's office, Tanya beeped the horn. John came out with an excited look on his face. He opened the car door and said, "Hi, son. Tanya, about this new case. I don't really like it, but it pays very well! No other lawyer in town has a deal this good! If word gets around, my client would not like that." He looked at Kirk. "Don't tell any of your friends."

"I won't, Dad! I would never do that. The subject bores me anyway."

"Well, Kirk!" said his mother with anger in her voice.

"I'm sorry if it bores you, son. I won't talk about it any more," John said, sounding pretty hurt.

"Sorry, Dad. Go on," Kirk said.

"Well, this guy and his partner were climbing Dare Mountain, the fools, and they couldn't decide which route to take, so they argued and my client pushed his partner off the mountain. Now has there ever been more of a fool?"

Dare Mountain? Kirk wondered if the TV news story had anything to do with his dad's new case.

When they got home, Kirk's mother ran out again to get Samantha, her one-year-old daughter, from the babysitter. She was back in fifteen minutes and Kirk had the table set and some macaroni and cheese on the stove, along with some chicken.

"Kirk, I hope Samantha grows up to be like you. You're almost always doing things without John or me having to tell you. You are *such* a sweetheart!"

They sat down to eat. They all bowed their heads—except Samantha who screamed, yelled, and then laughed—and said the grace: "Thank you, Lord, for our food. God bless us all." They said it in unison.

"Dad, could you tell us some more about the case with Dare Mountain now?" Kirk asked, shoving a piece of chicken in his mouth. "I'd like to climb that mountain some day."

"Don't be a fool," said his father.

"I'm not, Dad. I'm going to climb it."

"I don't want that mountain mentioned by you, Kirk, in this house ever again," said his mother sternly.

"But . . ." started Kirk.

"No. And that's final."

Kirk knew better than to argue.

Chapter 2
The Plan

Later, when Kirk was in bed, he started think-ing. He got up, got a piece of paper, and wrote:

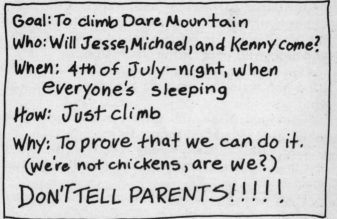

Goal: To climb Dare Mountain

Who: Will Jesse, Michael, and Kenny come?

When: 4th of July—night, when everyone's sleeping

How: Just climb

Why: To prove that we can do it. (We're not chickens, are we?)

DON'T TELL PARENTS!!!!!

Then he turned off the light. He'd tell the other guys tomorrow morning.

When he got up at 7:00, he used the phone that he had in his room to call Michael.

"Hi, Michael? I'm okay. How are you doing? Really? Hey, Michael, I have a plan. Come over now. You call Kenny and I'll call Jesse. Yes. Sure. You can sneak in the back door. Mom and Dad won't know. If they wake up? They won't care. Trust me. Yes. Well, call Kenny and I'll call Jesse. 'Bye."

He hung up the phone and then dialed Jesse's

number. "Hi, Jesse? Yeah. Sorry for calling so early, but I had to talk to you. Uh-huh. Yep. You've got it. All right. Well, come over here. The other guys are coming over too. Okay. 'Bye. HURRY!" He hung up the phone.

About ten minutes later his friends arrived at the door. He ran down the stairs to let them in.

"Hi, guys. Shh, my parents are sleeping. Come on upstairs," Kirk said when he opened the door. They quietly climbed up the stairs and went into Kirk's bedroom. He got the notebook off his desk, and brought it over for the others to see.

They read it. Then Michael said, "Puh-lease, Kirk. You actually think we can climb that? I'm out."

"Come on, Mike. You guys are coming, aren't you?" Kirk asked Kenny and Jesse.

"Gee, Kirk," said shy Kenny. "I don't think I want to climb it. After all, my papa did get killed on that mountain."

"How 'bout you, Jesse?" asked Kirk, knowing what the answer would be. "No. Right?"

"Actually, I think it's a good idea. I mean, I'm fourteen and my parents don't give me any freedom!" Jesse said. "It's a good idea, Kirk. I'm coming!"

"Really? You're such a good friend, Jesse. Michael must be chicken. Kenny, we can understand; his father died on that moun—"

He was interrupted by Kenny. "I'm coming too. Papa would be so proud of me if I did. So I guess I'll go!"

"Really, Kenny, if you don't want to, then—well—

you know. It was a dumb idea anyway," Kirk said, getting upset.

Kenny walked over to him and put his hand gently on Kirk's shoulder. "It's all right. It was a great idea. Come on. Let's make plans. We'll go, and we'll climb it. We'll make it, Kirk. Really, it's okay!"

"You don't mind? I was being kind of foolish, expecting to climb that thing. And even more, I expected you guys to *want* to come. I'm really sorry," Kirk replied, upset still, but feeling good because Kenny was a real friend.

They both sat down on Kirk's bed. Then Jesse came over and sat on the other side of Kirk. "We're a team!" all three said, and put their hands on top of each other's hands.

Then, slowly, Michael sat down next to the others. He said, "We're *all* a team!" as he added his hand to the pile. Kirk smiled. Then they all fell back and laughed.

They heard a knock on the door and sat up, suddenly remembering Kirk's parents.

"Yeah?" said Kirk.

"Kirk, What are you doing?"

"Oh! Mom!" Kirk said, getting up to let his mother in. "Sorry, Mom. I forgot you and Dad were still sleeping. I'm so sorry!" Kirk apologized.

His mom was holding Samantha with one arm. "That's okay, Kirk. You didn't wake me. Samantha did. Hi, boys! How are you? What are you doing here so early?" asked a very curious mother.

Kirk started to talk before his friends had a chance. "Mom, I invited them over here. I—uh—I had to get the, uh, homework assignment. Yeah.

And they all came over so we could, uh, study."

"Oh really? So you're not up to something? Good. I knew that my boy and his friends would not do anything bad. Am I right? Good. I sure don't want anything to happen to you little sweeties! Ta-ta!" she said as she left the room.

"Close call!" Kirk said. "Usually she asks me how much I've done, and wants to see it! She probably didn't want to embarrass me."

"Come on. We only have a few days to plan. What's today? The thirty-first? Omigosh! Five days! Let's plan, guys!" That was Michael.

They sat down and made these plans:

1. We all bring enough food for all of us. We don't sneak food without the other three knowing.
2. We all supply gear. If one of us has nothing, the other three of us share.
3. We will take two tents only. No more gear than we need.
4. Three outfits each. No more than what will fit in the packs along with the gear.
5. We will all agree on which route to take, and we will *not* hurt each other, at all, in any way, shape, or form!

"Gee, Kirk. Where'd you get that one?" asked Jesse.

"My father told me about—I mean, I just figured we wouldn't want to hurt each other. Right?" Kirk said. He'd almost spilled the beans! His father would have killed him! I know I can trust my friends! he thought to himself. But I had better not tell them.

They got back to the plans:

6. We will bring at least two first-aid kits, just in case.
7. We'll bring some *plastic* plates, cups, forks, knives, and spoons.
8. We have to bring simple food. We have to cook on campfires.
9. We can't bring milk. We can bring a kettle to make hot drinks.
10. Bring warm/cool clothes!! We can bring *one* sleeping bag each.

"If we think of anything else, we can add it to the list later," Jesse said.

"I'll be right back," said Kirk, moving towards the bathroom.

When he went in, Jesse whispered, "Hey, guys, let's hide on him! We'll jump out and scare him. Come on, let's shut off the lights!"

"Yeah!" They all agreed. They all hid. Jesse behind a chair, Kenny under the bed, and Michael wedged in between the bathroom door and the wall.

When Kirk stepped out, he walked over to turn on the lights. Before he could get past the bathroom door, Michael jumped out. "RAAR!" Michael yelled.

Kirk jumped a mile high! "You jerk!" Kirk yelled,

"That's all I can think of!" Michael said.

"Me too," Kenny agreed.

laughing as he jumped on top of Michael.

"I have to go now," said Kenny, coming out from under the bed. "My sister is going shopping with my mom, and I have to take care of Joshua. He thinks he can take care of himself, but he can't."

"Hey, Ken," Michael asked, "how old is Joshua?"

"Joshua's nine," said Kirk. "Don't you know anything about Kenny? I mean, I know a lot about him." Although all of them were friends, Kenny only really talked to Kirk. Kirk liked to listen to people. The others were more comedians and talkers than listeners.

"Well, I have to go now," said Jesse. "It's getting late."

"Me too. Mom and Dad will be MAD if I'm not back in time for lunch!" said Michael.

When they were all gone, Kirk lay down and thought . . . and planned. He would do it. He had to!

Chapter 3
The Climb

July 4th was here! This was the first time Kirk, Jesse, Kenny, and Michael weren't in the parade. They were busy up in Kirk's room, packing. Kirk told his parents that he had a headache, so they let him stay and watch the parade out the window.

The four boys had changed their plans. They were going to sneak off during the parade, while everyone was busy, either selling lemonade and cookies or watching the parade. They were going to use the back route through the woods. They could walk the three miles to the mountain.

The food they packed was basic, along with some cookies and candy bars, just in case they needed a snack. They also packed lots of juice and water.

They finished packing. "Here goes nothing," Kirk mumbled as he started out the door with the other three following. They sneaked into the woods. They ran until they couldn't hear or see anyone. But they ran slowly, because of the packs. The strongest ones, Michael and Kirk, had the tents.

They had walked two and a half miles already. They had half a mile left, and then they would be there. Dare Mountain!

They were actually going to climb it! They couldn't believe that they were going to climb Dare Mountain!

They walked for about another fifteen minutes, and there ahead of them was the place, the only place that there was for four fourteen-year-olds who needed to be away from their families for a little while.

They started up the mountain. They all knew the beginning of the climb would be just plain grassland, about eight miles of it, before they would get to the real tough part, the rocks. They'd probably spend about a week on the grassland. They had a month's worth of food, and they could probably stretch it out for another two or three weeks if they had to.

About four hours passed. They walked real slow, stopping a lot, still trying to decide if they should keep going. They decided that they would. They'd show everybody. They'd make it to the top. They'd name this mountain.

It was getting dark. "Hey, you guys, can we rest now?" Kenny asked, looking at his watch. "It's 8 o'clock now. We have to get up at dawn. Let's get some sleep. Please?"

"Okay. Let's get the tents up," said Kirk.

"I couldn't agree more," Michael said.

"All right. Let's get these tents up. The one I supplied holds three people," Jesse said.

"The one I supplied holds two people. So we'll sleep two to a tent. It will be safer and warmer that way," said Kirk.

They put up the tents and spread out their sleeping bags. They made a fire and put the rack they brought on top of it. They put on some frozen hamburgers that they had packed for their first night. They also had macaroni and cheese from a can as a side course.

They each found a rock and sat on it. They ate without conversation, so they could finish quickly and go to sleep.

They decided that Michael and Jesse would be in one tent, and Kenny and Kirk would be in the other. They decided this because Kenny and Kirk were more alike, and the same for Michael and Jesse.

When Kenny was almost done eating, he spotted a small deer. He got up and walked slowly towards it. Kenny loved nature, and it loved him.

"Kenny, where are you going?" asked Jesse.

But all Kenny did was put his hand up in a "one-minute" signal. The other three saw the deer then, and they knew that Kenny knew what he was doing. So Kenny kept on walking and he finally made it over to the deer. It didn't even try to run

away! He gently patted its head and pointed to the
spot behind the tree where the mother deer was
hiding. The small deer nodded its head, as if to say
yes, thank you; then it ran over to its mother.
Together they ran off through the woods. Kenny
always felt happy when he did something good for
nature. The other three boys stood up and clapped.

"You guys. Please. That was nothing. I just saw
this helpless little deer that couldn't find its
mother," Kenny said. They all walked over to their
tents and settled in to sleep.

The next morning Kenny woke up at 4:30. He
went over to a little stream that was nearby. He was
washing his face when all of a sudden he saw
something small and white floating in the water.
He picked it up, curious. Oh, yes, he recognized
what it was all right! "AAAAAAAGH!" he screamed,
loud, the loudest scream that Kirk, Jesse, or
Michael had ever heard! They all came running
and found Kenny crying.

"What's wrong?" they all asked. Kenny sobbed
and showed them the small white bone that he had
found in the stream.

"It's a human bone! We studied human bones
two months ago in school, and that is a finger
bone!" Kenny cried, panicked.

Kirk comforted him. "It's okay, Kenny. It'll be all
right."

"Yeah, Kenny. We're all here. It's really okay," said
Jesse and Michael. "Come on. Let's eat something
for breakfast."

"I'm not hungry!" Kenny said. Then he realized
what he was doing. "I'm sorry, guys! I didn't mean
it. It's just—that could be my papa's bone!"

Chapter 4
Poor, Poor Kenny

As they sat there, eating their dry cereal, they talked about how it would be to climb the rocks. They finished breakfast, packed, and made sure that the fire from the previous night was out. Then they started climbing. It was still grass-like, but they could see the *real* mountain now. Only about fifteen more minutes and they'd be there, on the rocks.

The fifteen minutes crawled by, as they trudged along with heavy packs behind them. But then, after what seemed like years, they made it, and they were ready for the ropes. They sat down and took out the ropes. Then they put the packs back on their backs. They each had a drink of water and a candy bar before their long journey ahead.

They made a hangman's noose knot and threw it up to the nearest ledge. It missed. They threw it again and still it missed. Kenny started walking around while Michael, Jesse, and Kirk took turns trying to get it on the ledge. Kenny was looking around and then he found a path-like place that led right to the ledge. He yelled, "Hey, guys, come here!"

"Kenny, we don't have time for deers right now!" yelled an ignorant Michael.

"It's not a deer. I found a way up!"

The next thing Kenny knew there were three curious boys looking where he was looking. Hot-shot Michael was the first to go over there. He climbed part way and saw that it was safe, so the other three followed. They walked up the little path as far as the ledge.

"Let's go this way," Jesse said, pointing at a rock that was formed into natural rock steps. They climbed up and came to a place where it was cut off by rocks. The only way to get onto the next ledge was to climb up it. There was nowhere they could put the rope, so they tried to climb without it. They fell each time.

"Maybe we should go home now," said Kenny.

"No. We can't give up. Not now. Who's the lightest here?" Kirk asked.

"Kenny is," said Jesse.

"Okay. Kenny, you try to climb up this rock. We'll be spotting you, and we won't let you get hurt. Honest. If you can get up there, you can tie this rope onto something and we'll climb up. Okay?" Kirk asked.

"Umm . . . I guess so. But—"

"Don't be wimpy, Kenny!" Michael said, cutting Kenny off.

Kirk defended him. "Hey! If Kenny doesn't want to, we know why. Now it's Kenny's choice. He's not a wimp either way."

"I'll go," Kenny said. "But I'll have to leave my pack down here. You guys can tie it onto the rope first and I'll pull it up."

"Yeah, okay. Now take this rope and climb up, or try anyway. Do the best you can. We have to get up there. There's no other way," Kirk said. He handed the rope to Kenny.

Kenny started up the mountain. Then he lost his hold. "AAAAAGH!" he screamed as he came tumbling down.

"OH NO! Catch him!" All three boys started yelling at once.

He landed in Jesse's arms and then he fell to the ground.

"Ouch," Kenny moaned. His head and arm were bleeding. Kirk was down to the ground in less than three seconds, digging the first-aid kit out of his pack. He found it and rushed to Kenny and applied a cream to his head and then a bandage. He took Kenny's shirt off because it started sticking to the blood. He washed the arm with some water out of his canteen.

"This might need stitches, guys," Kirk said. "But, if we can stop the bleeding we can just put on some bandages. Let's hope it's not too deep."

"Let's take him down to the hospital," Jesse said.

"No. We *have* to climb this mountain. He'll be fine!" Michael said.

"He can't finish climbing with a bad arm. He has to get to the hospital!" Jesse said.

"Why don't we wait and find out if he's all right. He's hurt. He might be okay and he might not. Now if you guys would stop arguing and please help me! Maybe we can stop his bleeding!"

They were sitting on the first ledge for about a half hour when Kenny finally came to.

"How do you feel?" Jesse asked.

"Fine. My head hurts a little bit."

"How's your arm? We stopped the bleeding. Do you feel the pain?" Kirk asked.

"My arm? What happened to it?"

"You fell, Kenny. Here, try to lift your pack," Kirk said. He had learned from his dad that if somebody hurt their arm they should try to lift something to see how weak they are.

Kenny took his pack. "Feels okay," he said. "Same as always."

The other three boys cheered.

"Let's go. We have to finish climbing the mountain," Kenny said, fitting his pack onto his back. The rest got their packs, and Kenny started up the rock again.

"You better not, Kenny. You'll get hurt!"

"No. I have to do this. It's the only way," he said. Clutching tightly to the rope he started up again. He slipped about halfway down, but then he went up again. Finally, he got up. He stood on the ledge and yelled, "HURRAY! You guys, look! I'm up!"

"What? Kenny? You made it? I don't believe it! You DID!" They were all shouting, looking up at him. Kenny walked over to a sharp rock that was sticking out and tied the rope onto the end, tightly. Then he took the other end of it and threw it down.

"I think my pack weighed me down so that I could get up!" Kenny shouted down.

"Good!" They all yelled. Then Michael, the strongest, tied the rope around his waist. Kenny pulled while Michael tried climbing up the moist walls of the rock. Michael was up after a while of struggling. Next Jesse went and Kirk was last.

When they got up, there were a million different ways to go.

"Michael and Kenny, why don't you go that way," Kirk said, gulping down water. "And Jesse and I will go this way." He pointed to where they would go. "In about an hour, we'll meet here again."

All four set their watches, right to the second.

"Why don't we go on different routes alone?" said Michael.

"Because if one of us gets hurt, nobody would know. So none of us will be alone, and we just hope nobody will be hurt," Jesse said thoughtfully.

"What if one of us falls? Do we call the other two or what?" Kenny asked.

"Definitely. Call the others if somebody falls. We *will* go home alive, all of us," Kirk said.

Then they all picked up their packs and started off on their routes.

Michael and Kenny were on their path when Kenny looked into the distance and saw a small bear cub. "Michael, do you see that?"

When Michael saw the cub he took out his hunting knife.

"No! You're not going to kill it! It's not going to hurt you! It's a harmless little baby!" Kenny shouted.

"Kenny, you are *such* a wimp! Why are you such a nature freak? You have to act like a man some time! You're fourteen years old and you are still afraid to kill a bear! When are you going to grow up?"

"Well, you're fourteen also, and you're so scared of a little bitty baby bear cub that you have to kill it! Are you such a wimp that you have to murder a poor little baby that's not even near you? Well, if that's the way men are suppose to act, then I guess I'm not one of them!"

"Ugh to you," Michael mumbled to himself. Suddenly Michael fell off the ledge. He caught onto a sapling and screamed.

"I'll get you, Michael. I'm not going to let you die! You are not going to fall, Michael! I won't let you. Please don't fall! Hold on! I can't have someone else that I care about die! Please don't!" Kenny screamed.

The others heard and started running. By the time they got there Kenny was trying to reach Michael.

"Michael, hold on! Grab my leg! I'll pull you up. Don't worry! I'll save you if it's the last thing I do!" Kenny shouted. He lowered himself down and Michael grabbed the rope that was hanging on Kenny's leg. Kenny pulled Michael up to the ledge and Michael climbed on. Kenny was still on the slippery part below. He lost his balance. "HELP ME! AAGH!" he screamed.

He was falling. DOWN! He'd be dead. Then the other boys were screaming. They did their best to save him, but he was out of sight.

"Kenny—NO! HE CAN'T BE DEAD! HE'S ALIVE! HE CAUGHT ONTO A LEDGE BELOW! *PLEASE!* This is a bad dream. He did not fall, did he, guys?" Michael screamed frantically.

"Michael," Jesse began. He was sobbing. "We have to accept it! It just happened!"

"No. It was all my fault. I should have watched what I was doing. Why? Why did Kenny have to die? It has to be my imagination. Kenny is not dead!"

"Hey, don't blame it on yourself. It wasn't your fault!" Kirk said, trying to reassure Michael. But then Kirk started to cry too.

"He never hurt anybody. He didn't even want to come, but we said it would be all right! Now he's

dead! We were wrong! I knew all the time that
something bad would happen. I knew it!" Kirk
screamed out. "What will his mom say? Poor
Kenny never did anything wrong. He was so good!"

"Please!" said Jesse. "Stop it! I may sound like I
don't really care, but, God, I do! Kenny cared about
everybody. He even risked his life to save Michael,
and they never got along too well. I loved him, and
I'll miss him; but if there is one thing I am not
going to do, it's quit. We made a deal that if something happened to one of us, we wouldn't quit.
Kenny would have been so proud if he could have
made it to the top. He'd be proud of us too. He's
saying, 'Go guys. Don't let my death stop you. Keep
going, please. Make it to the top,'"

Jesse said all this in a voice that trembled.

Chapter 5
The Victory

The days passed. Each of them had almost gotten killed, but the other two had saved them, and
still Kirk, Michael, and Jesse were brooding along.
They had passed most of the worst obstacles already, and were still trying to make it to the top.
They were out of food, except for some macaroni
and cheese and some beans. They had a few cans
of soup left also. Now that Kenny was gone, they
could kill small rabbits for food, but they decided
that it just wouldn't be right.

Then Jesse went off into the woods to see a big
rock and from there he could see the top of the
mountain.

"You guys! HEY, guys! I found a way up! Come

here!" The other two boys were there in a flash. They looked up. There it was. The top of the mountain. They would climb it. The three boys stood, amazed, looking into the sky. It had taken them one month and three days so far, and they hadn't found the way to the top.

"I wonder if they'll let us name it?" said Kirk.

"Yeah," Jesse said.

"I'd name it after Kenny. Give it his last name, since both he and his father lost their lives trying to climb it."

"Yeah," Jesse agreed.

"Yes. Of course. We could name it 'The Tackle Four,'" said Michael.

"No way. If we get to name it, we will call it 'Tackle Mountain,' just for Kenny, just his last name," Kirk said.

"Never mind. Let's climb. We have to get there before we name it," Jesse said, with his foot perched on top of a rock. They each took a drink of water and a piece of a Milky Way.

They climbed, and they climbed, slipping with each step they took. "Jesse, are you all right? Jesse? You're not hurt, are you?" Both boys eagerly said as Jesse slipped down the rock-slide that they had been climbing for the last forty-five minutes.

"Yeah, sure, I'm fine. Just bumped my head a little."

The two boys dropped the rope down to Jesse and held onto the other end. Jesse grabbed hold, and they pulled him up and up and up. Finally, they had Jesse right where he was before he had slipped. They climbed for another hour.

Then, there they were. They were standing on

the top of the mountain. Kenny's mountain—
Tackle Mountain. Whatever it would eventually be
named they were there, at the top of it.

As they admired the beauty around them, and
the world below them, they heard a noise coming
from above. "What's that? Omigosh! It's a helicopter!" The boys looked at each other.

Jesse was the first to say, "I don't believe it! It's
our parents!"

"What are we going to do? We have to make it
down again." said Kirk.

"I'm tired. Let's go with them," said Michael.

But Kirk was talking urgently. "No. We have to
finish. Going back down is part of climbing. It's
just as challenging and we need to do it. Maybe on
the way down we can find Kenny's body; then we
can have a proper funeral for him. Don't you think
it's worth it, guys? Don't you think it's possible?"
Kirk asked, just as the helicopter landed in front of
them.

Jesse ran over to his mom with tears in his eyes.
"Mom!" he cried.

Then Michael and Kirk spotted their parents getting out of the chopper, and they couldn't help but
run to give them loves.

"Oh, my baby. Oh, I missed you, Kirk. I thought
you were dead. Then I called your friends' parents
and their sons were gone too. We figured that you
went climbing because you were talking about it so
much, and your gear was gone, and . . . oh, Kirk,
I'm so glad we found you," Kirk's mother sobbed.
"Kirk, you are a terrible boy. Going off for almost
two months, worrying us like that."

"You little troublemaker, come here," his father

said. "You made it. You and your friends made it. We missed you, son, very much! So—what are you going to call it? Huh, boys?"

In that moment, Kenny's mother stepped forward.

"Boys," Kenny's mother began, "where's my son? Was he with you? Where is Kenny?" This was the question the boys were afraid of.

Kirk answered her. "Mrs. Tackle, I'm so sorry. I don't know how to tell you this . . . but . . ."

"Kenny's dead. Oh my God, Kenny can't be dead! He's out in the woods somewhere, right? Oh, please, say yes!" Kenny's mom begged.

"We're so sorry!" Kirk said.

They all cried for a long time.

"How did he . . . die?"

"He was saving Michael's life! Michael fell and Kenny went down to get him!" Kirk reported.

"That's not all. Kirk, Jess, I didn't tell you because you'd kill me," Michael said, trying to control his sobs. "There was this bear cub, and I was going to kill it. I was pretty scared of it. Kenny didn't want me to—"

"He always loved nature, and so did his papa," Mrs. Tackle cut him off.

"Yeah, we know. Well, he told me not to and so I called him—" Michael broke out in tears "—a wimp!"

"Kenny a wimp? No way, Michael!" Kirk said.

"I know. I guess I didn't want to admit that I was afraid. He said that I was the wimp if I was going to kill it and that was the only truth in that fight! I called him a nature freak. And, God, if I wasn't fighting I would have noticed where I was going.

But I didn't, and I fell. Kenny said he wasn't going to let anyone else he cared about die. And he saved my life! And I've hated myself ever since!"

"Oh, Michael, it's not your fault. Come here!" Kenny's mother cried. She gave him a big hug. "I know you tried to save him. I know it's not your fault. At least he died where his father did. He wanted to be so much like his papa. I am so proud of him!"

"Let me assist you to the helicopter," said Mr. Stinley, putting his arms around Mrs. Tackle. All the parents were climbing into the helicopter.

Jesse started to follow. "Jesse, aren't you going back down with us?" Kirk asked.

"Gee, guys, I don't know. I mean, I really miss my folks. I mean—"

"Yeah, I know what you mean," said Michael. "Hey Kirk, I don't mean to put you on the spot, alone, or anything, but I just can't bear to go back down this mountain. It's filled with memories that I don't want to remember. I'm sorry, Kirk. I want to finish, but I really can't!" Michael said.

"Hey, boys, hurry up. We don't have all day!" the pilot shouted.

"Boys, come on! What's wrong with you? Come on, now. There's a man in here who wants to discuss what you are going to name this mountain," Kirk's father called out.

"Dad, I'm not coming! I have to finish!"

"What? You're on the top, Kirk! What do you mean you have to finish?"

"Daddy, going down is just as challenging. You see, when I start something, I have to finish it.

"But, Kirk, you could be killed!"

"Those are the chances, Dad. Well, see ya. Kiss Samantha for me."

"No, Kirk, wait! Get your butt in here. Now! We came here to find you and your friends. Now get in here or you'll be grounded for a month. Get in!"

Kirk started down the mountain. But he didn't get more than a few steps when his dad tackled him. He picked Kirk up, pack and all, and carried him to the helicopter.

He threw Kirk in and got in himself.

"Honey, please forgive us!" Kirk's mom hugged him.

The chopper started.

"Wait! We have to get Kenny's body. We *have* to!" All the boys yelled.

"We will," said Kirk's father. He spoke to the pilot. "Sam, go down the mountain and turn the headlights on, please."

They found Kenny's body on a ledge, to the right of the one that they had climbed.

"Looks like he died instantly. Thank God for that," Michael's father said.

The men picked him up. He was all bloody. Poor, poor Kenny. Mrs. Tackle couldn't take her eyes off him. She just stared and stared.

They put him in the copter and covered him with blankets. In fifteen minutes they were home.

Chapter 6
Kenny's Funeral

The funeral was sad. They buried him next to his papa's empty grave. Kenny's headstone read:

THE LORD HAS CHOSEN TO TAKE THIS LAD,
AND MAY HE REST IN HEAVEN.
THE LORD HAS CHOSEN TO TAKE THIS BOY.
DEAR KENNY, GOD BLESS YOUR SOUL!

To this the boys added:

WE CLIMBED IT, AND WE NAMED IT AFTER YOU:
TACKLE MOUNTAIN. AND IT IS ALSO NAMED FOR
YOUR DAD. LOVE FOREVER, KIRK STINLEY, MICHAEL
SUSQUAN, AND JESSE DILAGAN

They had that carved on the back of the stone. Their parents had paid for it. They said they didn't care how high the cost, if it was for Kenny.

The boys planted rosebushes and flowers. Kenny's grave, and his father's, were the best looking graves in the whole cemetery. They came every day with lots of flowers for the rest of the summer. By the end of the three weeks, the two graves were so filled they couldn't squeeze one more flower in!

September came and went. Jesse, Michael, and Kirk were back in school. They continued to visit Kenny's grave whenever they could.

The people at school couldn't believe what had happened. Many also went to the grave. Even people that didn't totally admire Kenny prayed at his grave.

Others have tried to climb Tackle Mountain, but so far nobody has made it. Will it ever be climbed again?

THE END

ABOUT
THE
AUTHORS

LUCI CRAWFORD, who wrote "A Wintery Day," was born in Moline, Illinois, April 27, 1978, and now lives in Reynolds, Illinois, where she attends Reynolds Grade School. She collects unicorns and likes to draw.

☆

JOHN MARIO DEMASI, the author of "My Trip to School," was born June 9, 1978, in Morgantown, West Virginia, where he still lives and is a student at St. Francis DeSales Grade School. Some of his interests are reading, music, swimming, and collecting comic books. He likes to create original designs, and hopes to be an architect.

☆

IAN B. DEMERITT, who wrote "Angel," was born May 12, 1976, in Rochester, New York, and lives now in Luray, Virginia, where he goes to Mount Carmel Christian Academy. He enjoys writing stories and reading; and he has a special interest in astronomy and collects space posters. He would like to be an airplane pilot or an astronaut.

☆

J. J. DONOHUE was born in Oak Park, Illinois, April 17, 1977, and now lives in Wheaton, Illinois, where he attends Edison Middle School. At the time he wrote "My Fishy Friends" he was a student at Whittier School in Wheaton. He enjoys traveling, and spending time with his friends and his family; and he likes all kinds of sports—including, of course, fishing. He hopes some day to play professional sports.

J. S. ELDRIDGE, who wrote "Brotherly Love," was born October 11, 1976, in Reno, Nevada, and now lives in Elk Grove, California. He is a student at Florin Christian Academy in Sacramento, California. He likes to increase his knowledge about cars, and wants to be a marine biologist.

☆

MICHIKO HANAO was born in Hyōgo, Japan, December 1, 1976, and now lives in Tenafly, New Jersey, where she goes to Tenafly Middle School. She was attending Malcolm S. Mackay School in Tenafly when she wrote "Awful Day." She likes reading novels and collecting stuffed animals, and wants to be a TV interviewer.

☆

ANDREW ERIC HARRISON was born August 14, 1979, in Boston, Massachusetts. Now he lives in Barrington, Rhode Island, where he attends Middle Highway Elementary School. When he wrote "The Talking Iguana" he was a student at Hampden Meadows School in Barrington. He likes video games, skateboarding, riding his bike, drawing, and reading. Some of his ambitions are to be a comedian, an artist, and maybe a writer.

☆

CHRIS JOPLIN, the author of "The Weirdest Dream of My Life . . . Part III," was born September 3, 1975, in West Plains, Missouri, where he still lives and attends West Plains Middle School. He likes swimming, basketball, and golf, and playing Nintendo, and he *loves* pizza. He wants to go to the University of Missouri at Columbia, major in engineering, and play N.B.A. basketball.

☆

EILEEN MARKEY, the author of "Kate Did It," was born April 2, 1976, in Holyoke, Massachusetts, and now lives in Springfield, Massachusetts, where she is a student at Holy Cross School. Her interests include Irish step-dancing, playing the violin, and collecting dollhouse miniatures. She hopes to be a writer of books for young teenage readers, and to live on the coast of Maine.

☆

JOHNNY QUIÑONES, who wrote "The Farmer's Choice," was born September 27, 1975, in Corpus Christi, Texas, where he still lives and attends Vicente Lozano Special Emphasis School. Some of his interests are making models, playing football, skateboarding, and fishing. His ambitions are to be a football player and a game warden.

☆

RON RISKE, JR., the author of "Days on the Bus," lives in Port Lavaca, Texas, where he was born April 22, 1978, and is a student at Jackson Elementary School. He likes video games, drawing, and playing the piano; and he enjoys sports, including 4-H shooting sports and trampolining.

NAOMI ANNE SCHAEFER was born Febraury 24, 1977, in Worcester, Massachusetts. She still lives there and goes to Forest Grove Junior High. At the time she wrote "Growing Up" she was a student at Solomon Schechter Day School in Worcester. She is a team swimmer, and likes dancing and is a serious ceramicist. She would like to be a writer of both fiction and nonfiction for children.

☆

AMANDA J. SULLIVAN was born in Newton, Massachusetts, October 12, 1976, and now lives in Rumney, New Hampshire. She goes to Newfound Memorial High School in Bristol, New Hampshire. When she wrote "They Called It Dare Mountain" she was a student at Bristol Elementary School. Some of her interests are babysitting, acting, reading, and writing; and she would like to become an actress and a writer.

HONORABLE MENTIONS

The work of these one hundred and fifteen young writers received honorable mention in the Young Authors of America Contest:

Matthew Aldrich, Plymouth, NH
Mike Alton, Acworth, GA
Heather Ballestad, Green Bay, WI
Leigh Ann Bartlett, Baltimore, MD
Tiffany Barttrum, Muncie, IN
Anne Berenbom, Overland Park, KS
Kelly Bluteau, San Antonio, TX
Corey Bregman, Skokie, IL
Jennifer Brewington, Petal, MS
Benjamin Don Carter, Petal, MS
Matthew F. Cary, Philadelphia, PA
Jessica Casaletto, Alexandria, VA
Chris Cline, Bellingham, WA
Consuelo Diaz, Los Angeles, CA
Sean Donley, San Antonio, TX
Christy Drouillard, Tulsa, OK
Shauna Durhman, Chatfield, MN
Kyle FitzGerald, Lemon Grove, CA
Danny Forrest, Homer, AK
Chris Franzen, Breckenridge, CO
Jason Fugate, Houston, TX
Adam Galeen, Baldwin, NY
Geoffrey Scott Gelb, St. Louis, MO
Timothy J. Geroux, Oswego, NY
Lois Gicas, Tenafly, NJ
Tosca Gilblom, Saugus, CA
Ned Greer, River Hills, WI

Jonathan Greulich, Woodville, OH
Chad Grider, Columbia, PA
Jennifer Groner, Jacksonville, FL
Matthew Harding, Wilmington, OH
Samiko Hashimoto, Closter, NJ
Gina Herro, Mogadore, OH
Beth Herzog, Brooklyn, NY
Evan Hume, Lawrenceville, NJ
Chelsea Jackson, Coram, NY
Sarah Jaraczeski, Cheyenne, WY
Shannon Kearney, West Chester, PA
Kelly Kendrick, Hamilton Square, NJ
Tim Kraus, Cincinnati, OH
Adam Krupp, Plymouth, IN
Kyle Kuhn, Dunkerton, IA
Kyra Kyles, Chicago, IL
Molly Lacher-Katz, Barrington, RI
Sarah Leffler, Charlottesville, VA
Emily MacDonald, Knoxville, TN
Cory Maglinger, Owensboro, KY
Joey L. Martinez, Woodlake, CA
Vered Metson, Newton, MA
Larry A. Mills, Chicago, IL
Amy Mix, Chisago City, MN
Sara E. Monroe, Lexington, KY
Becky Moore, Rockland, ME
Sally Morris, Sturgis, MI
Aaron Musgrave, Fairfield, IL
Kate Neville, Corvallis, OR
Gwen Newman, West Chester, PA
Kevin Parker, Canterbury, NH
Shayna Parker, Bingham, ME
Scott Parkinson, McLean, VA
Julie Lauren Pelc, Milwaukee, WI
Jennifer Peterson, Plymouth, MI
Robert Pomorski, Warren, MI
Marnie Randall, Westbrook, ME
Meg Randall, Westbrook, ME
Jayme Reaves, Russellville, KY
Natalie Recker, Vinton, IA
Owein Reese, Mendham, NJ
LaRae Reier, Union City, OH
Nicole Richardson, San Leandro, CA
Jason Rinderle, Cincinnati, OH
Thomas Rizzo, Closter, NJ

Adam Roach, El Reno, OK
Justin Roberts, Des Moines, IA
Marnie Sue Santaniello, York, PA
Nishi Sarda, Houston, TX
Joe Schmulbach, Taylor Ridge, IL
Kenneth Seger, North Chicago, IL
Jessica Smarsch, Rochester Hills, MI
Todd Snead, Georgetown, TX
Stefanie Spillers, Des Moines, IA
Michell Stanley, Cincinnati, OH
Brandon Stansbury, Redmond, WA
Trevor Stevenson, Victor, ID
Tommy Stocky, St. Louis, MO
Kerrin Strevell, Valatie, NY
Anna Sugden-Newbery, Madison, WI
Alison Sweeney, Rockford, IL
Cory Tanguay, Scarboro, ME
Julie Marie Tate, Clarkston, WA
Christina Terrazas, Englewood, CO
Michelle Thomas, Tempe, AZ
Emily Thurston, Princeton, NJ
Bradley Townsley, Englewood, CO
Andy Trujillo, Schererville, IN
Putnam R. Trumbull, Okemos, MI
Clinton Tsurui, Fremont, CA
Alex Turcotte, Medford, NJ
Shawn Valentine, Blanchester, OH
Eric Vazquez, Detroit, MI
Robert Ver Straten, Coram, NY
Aaron Villa, Laveen, AZ
Huong Viet Vu, Auburn, CA
Kevin Walker, Springville, UT
Matthew Walton, Wilmington, NC
Jessica Ward, Carlisle, PA
Becki Warden, Orem, UT
David Wargo, Boise, ID
Daniel Warner, Manchester, MO
Teddy Weldon, Placerville, CA
David Weremay, Seekonk, MA
Jesse Wiitala, Jacobson, MN
Phylicia Woullard, Hattiesburg, MS
Joseph Wu, Lexington, KY
Alan Zelenka, Prairie City, OR